Discover & Learn

Anglo-Saxons

Years 5-6

This Teacher Book is the perfect companion to CGP's
'Anglo-Saxons' Activity Book for Years 5-6.

It contains a range of useful resources, including answers,
information for teachers, prompts and guidance for pupils,
and suggestions for extension activities.

It's ideal for helping your pupils explore the KS2 History topic
'Britain's settlement by Anglo-Saxons and Scots'.

The Fall of the Roman Empire

Anglo-Saxons: Activity Book p.2-3

2

The Fall of the Roman Empire

The Romans ruled most of Europe for over 400 years. But by AD 410 their western Empire was starting to collapse. Now read pages 2 and 3 of the Study Book.

In your own words, say why you think that the western Roman Empire collapsed.

The western Roman Empire collapsed because it had grown so big that it could not afford to pay the soldiers it needed to defend itself from invaders.

Many of the tribes that invaded the Roman Empire were <u>nomads</u>.

What are nomads? Use page 2 of the Study Book to help you.

Nomads are people who don't settle in one place but travel around instead.

The nomadic tribes lived in tents that they could carry around with them.

This picture shows what a nomad's home might have looked like.

Would you rather live like a Roman or like a nomad? Use the image above and what you know about how the Romans lived to explain your answer.

I would rather live like a ....

because ....

....

....

Pupil Guidance:
"Think about how both nomads and Romans lived. If you were a nomad, you would have to carry everything you needed with you. Romans lived in one place in stone houses."

Extension Idea
Pupils could compare their lives now with the lives of nomads and Romans. Pupils could then decide whether their lives are more like the lives of Romans or nomads.

Pupils can say that they would rather live like a nomad or like a Roman, as long as they support their decision with a good reason.

The Fall of the Roman Empire: National Curriculum Aims

- Understand abstract terms such as 'empire'.
- Understand how empires are dissolved.
- Know about the history of the wider world.
- Understand why there are different interpretations of the past.

3

Use page 3 of the Study Book to find out if these statements are <u>true</u> or <u>false</u>. Tick the correct box for each statement.

Vandals and Huns invaded the Roman Empire.   True ✓   False ☐

The Huns came from Germany.   True ☐   False ✓

The invaders probably liked the way the Romans lived.   True ☐   False ✓

The invaders might have wanted more space to live in.   True ✓   False ☐

Extension Idea

Higher ability pupils could be asked to write out true versions of the false sentences.

We can use Roman texts to find out what the invaders might have been like.

Circle the words below that you think the Romans would have used to describe the invaders.

(Violent)   Polite   (Dangerous)

                              Friendly

Peaceful   Calm   (Scary)   Civilised

Pupil Guidance:

"Think about how the Romans described Attila the Hun (page 3 of the Study Book)."

Extension Idea

Pupils could be encouraged to think of some words that the invaders might have used to describe the Romans.

Do you think the invaders were really how the Romans described them? Circle your answer in the sentence below, then explain why you think this.

I think the invaders probably   did / didn't   match the Roman's

descriptions of them because ....

....

....

"I understand the reasons for the fall of the western Roman Empire, and the rise of the Vandals and Huns." 👍✓ ✊✓ 👎✓

Pupils can select either answer, as long as their choice is supported by a good reason. The best answers might say that the invaders did not match the Romans descriptions of them because the Romans were <u>biased</u> against the invaders.

Extension Idea

Ask pupils to look at the pictures of Rome and imagine they were a Hun or a Vandal seeing the city for the first time. What would they notice? Would anything scare them? Would they want to live there?

The Romans Leave Britain

There are many possible answers here, though most pupils should identify that it would have been <u>scary</u> or <u>worrying</u> to be a Roman during this time because of the barbarian attacks.

Pupil Guidance:

"Look at the picture of Attila the Hun on page 3 of the Study Book, or the painting of the barbarians on page 4, to see how other artists think the barbarians might have looked."

Any image is acceptable, as long as pupils use their labels to justify why they have drawn their picture the way they have.

4

The Romans Leave Britain

The Romans withdrew from Britain in AD 410. They needed their troops to fight the people invading Roman cities in western Europe.

Read page 4 of the Study Book. How do you think it felt to be a Roman in AD 410? Explain your answer.

....

....

....

The Romans called the invaders 'barbarians'.

Draw a picture of what you think a barbarian might have looked like. <u>Label</u> your barbarian to explain why you have drawn him or her the way you have.

The <u>Vandals</u> were one of the tribes the Romans called barbarians.

Imagine you're a Vandal. Write a few sentences explaining why it's unfair that the Romans have called you and your friends barbarians.

Look back at page 4 of the Study Book to find out more about the Vandals and barbarians.

I think it's unfair that the Romans call us barbarians because <u>we do care about more than just fighting. We make beautiful jewellery like gold necklaces.</u>

Pupils should engage with the fact that the barbarians were <u>skilled craftsmen</u> and had a <u>culture</u> — there is archaeological evidence that supports this in the form of the beautiful jewellery they made.

The Romans Leave Britain: National Curriculum Aims
- Understand how empires are dissolved.
- Understand change.
- Understand how Britain has been influenced by the wider world.
- Understand how evidence is used to make historical claims.

Read page 5 of the Study Book.

We don't have much written information about what life was like in Britain between AD 400 and AD 600. In your own words, explain why.

There are very few written records about what life was like in Britain between AD 400 and AD 600 because the tribes that invaded the Roman Empire in this period didn't keep historical records.

Extension Idea

Without written records, it can be hard to work out exactly what went on during this dark age. Pupils could discuss what other forms of evidence historians could use to find out about this period of history.

Use page 5 of the Study Book to find out if these statements are true or false. Tick the correct box for each statement.

Constantinople was a city in Turkey. True ✓ False

Constantinople was conquered by the barbarians. True False ✓

Constantinople helped to keep Christianity alive in Britain. True ✓ False

Christian monks wrote about British history. True ✓ False

Higher ability pupils may write that the tin should be Cornish or from Cornwall.

Imagine you're a trader from Constantinople. Draw a picture of something you might want to trade with the Britons. What would you like to get from the Britons in return? Use page 5 of the Study Book to help you.

I would like to trade this item for tin

Extension Idea

Pupils could discuss trade in modern day Britain and explore things that we might export or import. For example, we import food we can't grow ourselves.

"I understand what happened when the western Roman Empire collapsed and the Romans left Britain."

Extension Idea

Pupils could split up into groups to trade for classroom items. They could be encouraged to decide how much the different items are worth and what they'd be willing to trade each item for.

Suggested Scaffolding:
Pottery from Turkey was found in Britain.

Writing About Britain

Anglo-Saxons: Activity Book p.6-7

6

Writing About Britain

Historians find it hard to know exactly what happened in Britain between AD 400 and 600. Some of what we do know was written by the monks Gildas and Bede.

Read pages 6 and 7 of the Study Book. The statements below describe <u>Gildas</u>, <u>Bede</u> or <u>both Gildas and Bede</u>. Write them out in the correct columns in the table. The first one has been done for you.

Was born around AD 500   Was a monk   Was writing in AD 730

Wrote from a Christian viewpoint   Wrote about British history   Wrote using lots of other sources from Europe

Wrote about things that happened before he was born

Gildas	Bede	Both
Was born around AD 500	Was writing in AD 730 \ \ Wrote using lots of other sources from Europe	Was a monk \ \ Wrote from a Christian viewpoint \ \ Wrote about British history \ \ Wrote about things that happened before he was born

Why did Gildas think bad things happened to people in Britain?

He thought the Britons were being punished by God for the bad things that they had done.

Extension Idea

Gildas and Bede both wrote about events that happened <u>before</u> they were born. Pupils could discuss how Gildas and Bede might have found out about past events, and how modern day historians might find out about the recent and distant past.

Pupil Guidance:

"Remember that Gildas wrote from a Christian point of view."

Extension Idea

Pupils could stain some thick paper with tea, dry it and press it, and then write a <u>historical account</u> of something that has happened locally. Remind them that they can use <u>magic</u> as the explanation for things that have happened. And if something bad has happened, it must be because someone has sinned!

Writing About Britain: National Curriculum Aims
- Understand the methods of historical enquiry.
- Understand how evidence is used to make historical claims.
- Create structured accounts.

7

How did Bede try to make his work reliable?

Reliable means trustworthy and accurate.

Bede tried to base his work on lots of different sources and check the sources that he used.

Higher ability pupils may refer to Bede using sources from <u>Europe</u> as well as Britain.

The Anglo-Saxon Chronicle is a <u>timeline</u> of events that were important in British history from 60 BC to AD 1154.

Read this list of events from the Chronicle.

> AD 514 — A group of Saxons arrived in Britain with three ships.
> AD 538 — There was an eclipse of the sun.
> AD 588 — King Ella of Northumbria died.
> AD 592 — Gregory became the Pope in Rome.
> AD 646 — King Kenwal was baptised.

Imagine you are writing a Chronicle for modern-day Britain. Chose some important events, along with the years they happened, to go into your Chronicle.

You can write the year 2014 as AD 2014. It means the same thing.

AD *2012 — Queen Elizabeth II celebrated her Diamond Jubilee.*

AD *2012 — Britain hosted the Olympic games in London.*

AD *2013 — Andy Murray won the Wimbledon men's tennis title.*

AD *2014 — The referendum for Scottish independence was held.*

"I know about some of the important writers and texts from post-Roman Britain."

Suggested Scaffolding:
Pupils could write about:
- Political events
- Major news stories
- Events involving the Royal family
- Major sporting events

Pupils could discuss and share ideas for events before starting the task.

Extension Idea
Pupils could be given an event or news story from modern Britain to research. They could put together an account of the event using different sources. Pupils could compare accounts of the same event to see if they vary.

A wide range of answers is possible for this question. Pupils should report events relevant to <u>Britain</u> and try to give the years accurately.

Life After the Romans

Anglo-Saxons: Activity Book p.8-9

8

Life After the Romans

The Romans had been responsible for running Britain for over 400 years.
When they left, a lot of the industry that they'd set up disappeared.
Between around AD 400 and AD 600, hardly any coins were produced in Britain.

List <u>two</u> things that you could buy with coins in Britain today.

1) *sweets / clothes / cinema tickets / toys / books /*

2) *games / DVDs / music / magazines*

List <u>two</u> things that you think a Briton in AD 410
might have wanted to buy with coins.

1) *food / material to make clothes / land / farming tools /*

2) *animals / jewellery / pottery / slaves*

There were fewer coins in Britain after the Romans had gone,
so Britons had to buy and sell items in different ways.

What do you think Britons could have done instead of using coins?

Instead of using coins, I think the Britons could have
traded different items with each other.

Read page 8 of the Study Book. In your own words, explain why
new coins stopped being made in Britain after the Romans had gone.

New coins stopped being made in Britain after the
Romans had gone because there was no one left in
Britain who was able to run the mines and make coins.

Pupil Guidance:

"Think about what Britons in AD 410 might have needed to survive. What items would have been available to them?"

Extension Idea

Pupils could discuss similarities and differences between things they could buy now and things Britons might have bought in AD 410. Why do these similarities and differences exist?

Some Roman coins had bits snipped off, sometimes so much that only the emperor's face showed, with nothing round it. Bits cut off real coins could be use to make false coins to add to the supply.

Higher ability pupils may refer to <u>minting</u> coins.

Life After the Romans: National Curriculum Aims

- Know the history of Britain as a chronological narrative.
- Understand similarity and difference and use them to draw contrasts.
- Understand change.

9

Buildings in Britain changed after the Romans left.
This photograph shows the remains of a Roman building in Cumbria.

These are the remains of a bath house at Ravenglass Roman fort in Cumbria. The bath house is one of the tallest Roman ruins still surviving in Britain today. The fort was built in the 2nd century AD.

What is the building in the photo made of? Tick <u>one</u> box.

wood ☐   stone ☑

Read page 9 of the Study Book. What would a building that was built after the Romans left be made of? Why?

It would be made of *wood*

because *the people in Britain were not organised enough*

to quarry the stones needed to build stone buildings.

Extension Idea
Pupils could discuss why they think we have more ruins of stone buildings than of wooden buildings in Britain.

Read the statements below and decide whether they are <u>true</u> or <u>false</u>. Tick the correct box for each statement.

Roman magistrates were still in Britain in AD 600.   True ☐ False ☑

Law and justice struggled to survive
after the Romans left Britain.   True ☑ False ☐

Christianity stopped in Britain
as soon as the Romans left.   True ☐ False ☑

Christianity kept Roman culture going in Britain.   True ☑ False ☐

"I understand the ways in which life changed for
the Britons once the Romans left Britain."

The First Invasions

Anglo-Saxons: Activity Book p.10-11

The First Invasions

Even before the Romans left, Britain was attacked by <u>invaders</u> from other countries. Read page 10 of the Study Book.

In the table below, write down the names of <u>three tribes</u> that were attacking Britain before the Romans had left. Write down <u>where</u> each tribe was from. The name of the first tribe has been done for you.

Tribe	Where from
Scots	Ireland
Picts	north Britain
Saxons	Europe

The <u>Angles</u> and the <u>Jutes</u> also attacked Britain from Europe.

Gildas wrote that a leader called <u>Vortigern</u> invited the Saxon armies over to Britain to help fight off the invaders. Legend says that an army was led by the brothers <u>Hengist</u> and <u>Horsa</u>.

Imagine you're <u>Vortigern</u>. Write a letter to Hengist and Horsa asking them to come to Britain. Say why you want their help and what you'll give them in return.

Use page 10 of the Study Book to help you.

Dear Hengist and Horsa,

I really need your help fighting the Picts and the Scots who are invading us. Since the Romans left, we are not strong enough to defend ourselves. If you come and help us fight them, I will pay you and give you land to settle on in the south-east of Britain.

Suggested Scaffolding

"You might want to include these words in your answer:
- *Picts*
- *Scots*
- *fight / defend*
- *land / money"*

Extension Idea

Pupils could pretend to be Hengist or Horsa and write a letter in reply to Vortigern. They could include questions the brothers might have had, as well as any other demands.

Extension Idea

Pupils could research the history of St Patrick — a Romano-British boy captured and enslaved by Irish raiders. They could write the story of how he became Ireland's patron saint.

The First Invasions: National Curriculum Aims

- Know the history of Britain as a chronological narrative.
- Understand cause and consequence.
- Create written narratives and structured accounts.
- Understand why there are different interpretations of the past.

11

If you were Vortigern, would you have asked the Saxons for help?
Why or why not? If not, what might you have done instead?

....

....

....

Either answer is acceptable here. Pupils may say that they <u>would</u> have asked the Saxons for help because they were worried about the Picts and the Scots. Or they may say that they <u>wouldn't have trusted</u> the Saxons, given their past attacks on Britain, and that they would have asked someone else for help instead.

According to Gildas, the Saxons worked for Vortigern,
but soon <u>rebelled</u> against him and the Britons.

Read page 11 of the Study Book. Now imagine you're <u>Hengist</u>. Write down your reasons for rebelling against the Britons in the speech bubble below.

Hengist

I rebelled against the Britons because they were weak and cowardly. I knew we could defeat them easily in battle. I didn't like it when Vortigern refused to give us more land for helping him, so I decided to take land for myself.

Pupil Guidance:

"What is Hengist supposed to have thought the Britons were like? Why might he have been angry with Vortigern?"

Gildas wrote that the Saxon rebellion was violent. Historians think he might have made the Saxons sound <u>worse</u> than they really were.

Can you think why Gildas might have done this?

I think Gildas might have done this because he didn't like the Saxons / he was angry with the Saxons.

Gildas was writing after the events he describes had taken place. By this point, the Anglo-Saxons controlled large areas of Britain and Gildas wasn't happy about it.

"I know about the invasions of Britain that took place around the start of the 5th century."

Extension Idea

Pupils could split up into groups and put on a play about how the Saxons came to Britain. Pupils could take on the roles of Vortigern, Hengist, Horsa and the Saxon armies. 'Gildas' could even narrate!

Britain Fights Back

Anglo-Saxons: Activity Book p.12-13

Suggested Scaffolding:

"On your poster, you should include:

- *A title*
- *A picture of what a leader might look like.*
- *A sentence describing what your leader will need to do.*
- *A sentence describing what your leader should be like. You might want to include words like 'brave', 'clever' or 'strong'."*

Suggested Scaffolding:

Pupils could be given statements or slogans to build their posters around, for example: 'Lead us into battle!' or 'Think you've got what it takes? Show those Saxons who's boss!'

Pupils should have recognised that the poster is an <u>advert</u> and tried to make it as bright and eye-catching as possible, in order to attract attention. They should also have tried to use persuasive language.

12

Britain Fights Back

The Britons struggled to defend themselves against the Saxon invaders. They needed a <u>strong leader</u> to bring them together and lead them into battle.

Imagine you are part of a group of worried Britons from that time. Design a <u>poster</u>, advertising for someone to lead the Britons into battle against the Saxons.

> Think about what your leader will need to be like, and what they will have to do.

Read page 12 of the Study Book. The <u>Battle of Badon Hill</u> is thought to have been an important battle in early British history.

Tick the box below that best describes what happened at the Battle of Badon Hill.

The Saxons defeated the Britons. ☐

The Britons defeated the Saxons. ☑

The Saxons defeated the Angles. ☐

The Angles defeated the Jutes. ☐

Britain Fights Back: National Curriculum Aims

- Understand methods of historical enquiry.
- Understand how evidence is used to make historical claims.
- Understand why there are different interpretations of the past.

13

Why don't we know much about the battles that happened in Britain around AD 500? Fill in your answer below.
You might want to use some of the key words from the box.

Key Words

written texts   *unreliable*
archaeological   *evidence*

We don't know much about battles that happened at this time because

there aren't many written texts about this period.
There's not much archaeological evidence either.

King Arthur is a popular legend. You might have heard some of the stories we tell about him today — like when he pulled a magical sword from a stone.

Read page 13 of the Study Book and decide whether the following statements are true or false. Tick the correct box for each statement.

King Arthur definitely existed.	True ☐	False ✔
King Arthur isn't mentioned in the Anglo-Saxon Chronicle.	True ✔	False ☐
Some people think King Arthur fought in the Battle of Badon Hill.	True ✔	False ☐
Gildas and Bede wrote about King Arthur.	True ☐	False ✔
The popular stories about King Arthur were written much later than AD 500.	True ✔	False ☐

"I know about how the Britons fought the Saxon invasions and about the legend of King Arthur."

Extension Idea
Pupils could discuss how we know about wars, battles or other events that take place today. They could talk about newspapers and television reports, as well as the role of social media.

Higher ability pupils may apply what they know about the nature of written texts from this time and also say that the texts we do have may be unreliable.

Extension Idea
The legend of Arthur is still told in modern times. Pupils could research how Arthur is portrayed today, in television, films or books. They could then discuss the ways in which he is made to appear as a hero.

Extension Idea
Around 536 AD, a piece of Halley's Comet is thought to have introduced a raft of dust into the Earth's atmosphere which cooled the Earth and caused drought and famine. Ask pupils to consider why famine might result in a change in leadership of the country, and maybe lead to invasions by hostile forces.

Becoming Anglo-Saxon

Anglo-Saxons: Activity Book p.14-15

Pupils' maps may vary, but should show roughly this pattern.

Extension Idea

If the area where they live is shown, pupils could try to locate it on this map. Which tribe was in control of the area in AD 550?

Extension Idea

Higher ability pupils could draw what they think the new map might look like.

A part of Roman life that did not survive for long after the Anglo-Saxons arrived was the villa. They were too isolated, too vulnerable, and too difficult to keep going without lots of slaves.

14

Becoming Anglo-Saxon

By AD 550, different tribes had all claimed their own bits of land in Britain. Read page 14 of the Study Book.

This map shows part of Britain. Use colouring pencils to show where each of the tribes below settled. Fill in the key to show which colour you've used for each tribe.

Key:

☐ = Angles   ☐ = Picts

☐ = Saxons   ☐ = Scots

☐ = Britons   ☐ = Jutes

Where had the <u>Scots</u> tribe come from?
Circle the correct answer from the choices below.

(Ireland)   Scotland   Wales

Northern Europe   Africa

Tick the statement below that best describes how the map above would look by <u>AD 600</u>.

The Anglo-Saxon tribes would have moved further west.   ✔

The Britons would have moved further east.   ☐

The Anglo-Saxons kingdoms wouldn't have changed.   ☐

Extension Idea

Ask pupils to imagine they are an Anglo-Saxon child who has wandered away from their settlement and has come across a huge, empty building — in fact an <u>abandoned Roman villa</u>. Ask pupils to write (or plan and deliver orally) an adventure story based on their discovery.

Becoming Anglo-Saxon: National Curriculum Aims

- Know the history of Britain as a chronological narrative.
- Understand how Britain has been influenced by the wider world.
- Understand the connections between local and national history.
- Understand change.

15

One piece of evidence that tells us where the Anglo-Saxons settled in Britain is <u>place names</u> that come from Anglo-Saxon words.

Here are some Anglo-Saxon words and their meanings:

		<u>Meaning</u>
ley	=	a clearing in a wood
ford	=	a river crossing
ham	=	a village
stow	=	a holy/religious place

Here are some place names in England:

Oakley	Ashley
Altrincham	Chelmsford
Oxford	Padstow

From the place names in the box above, can you find:

A town that used to be a village — _Altrincham_

A town that used to be a holy place — _Padstow_

A place that used to be a clearing in an oak wood — _Oakley_

A place where oxen could cross the river — _Oxford_

Read page 15 of the Study Book. Fill in the speech bubble below to explain why a Saxon farmer might have wanted to settle in Britain.

A Saxon Farmer

I want to settle in Britain because _the area where I live is very bad for farming. It always floods! Britain has very fertile land so is perfect for farming and growing crops._

"I understand when, where and why the Anglo-Saxons might have settled in Britain."

Extension Idea

Pupils could look at some of the names of towns, cities or villages near them. They could use books or the Internet to research whether these names come from Anglo-Saxon words, and what each name means. Pupils may need help finding suitable websites.

Pupil Guidance:

"Why was the <u>land</u> in Britain <u>better</u> for a Saxon farmer than the land back home?"

Higher ability pupils may write that the area the Saxons came from was <u>flat land</u> in <u>northern Germany</u>.

Anglo-Saxon Settlements

Anglo-Saxons: Activity Book p.16-17

16

Anglo-Saxon Settlements

Most Anglo-Saxons were farmers who lived in small villages.

Read page 16 of the Study Book.

If we wanted to eat some vegetables, we could just go to a shop and buy them.

How would an Anglo-Saxon get vegetables to eat?

They would grow their own vegetables or trade their skills for them.

Read page 17 of the Study Book.

West Stow is an Anglo-Saxon settlement that has been rebuilt in modern times.

What are the houses at West Stow made from?
Circle five correct materials below.

(Wood)   (Mud)   (Animal dung)   Metal

Bricks   Stone   (Hair)   (Straw)

This picture shows the inside of a house at West Stow.

What do you think living in an Anglo-Saxon house would be like? Why do you think this? Use the information on page 17 of the Study Book and this photo to help you.

I think living in an Anglo-Saxon house would have been uncomfortable because everything in the picture is made of wood. It would also have been crowded and smelly because often the whole family and their animals lived there together.

Pupil Guidance:

"Anglo-Saxon houses were very basic — the whole family would have all lived in one room. There would have been no electricity, no central heating and no running water."

Extension Idea

Pupils could be asked to draw their house and compare it to a house from West Stow. They could be encouraged to think about similarities and differences in building materials, structure, lighting, etc.

Any reasonable answer is acceptable here as long as pupils can justify it. The best answers will refer to both the picture and the Study Book.

Anglo-Saxon Settlements: National Curriculum Aims

- Know how people's lives have shaped Britain.
- Understand similarity and difference and use them to draw contrasts.

Anglo-Saxons sometimes kept their animals inside their houses.

Using page 17 of the Study Book, write down <u>two</u> reasons why they did this.

1) *To help to keep the house warm.*

2) *To keep the animals safe from wolves and bears.*

The king would often throw feasts in the great hall.

Fill in the table below to show the differences between an Anglo-Saxon feast and a modern-day party. Use the information on page 17 of the Study Book to help you.

	At an Anglo-Saxon feast	At a modern-day party
People would eat...	roast meats	crisps cake
People would drink...	mead beer	cola lemonade
People would listen to...	stories music played on a lyre	pop music
People might give these things as presents...	jewellery treasure	toys clothes

"I understand what life in an Anglo-Saxon house and village might have been like."

Extension Idea

"Imagine that you are part of a Romano-British family living in a small village. A group of Saxons come and settle nearby. To start with, they keep themselves to themselves, but one day, a man comes seeking the services of your healing woman. His wife is having a baby and needs help. Some people in your village feel she shouldn't go and help them, but you have been looking forward to the opportunity to meet new children to play with. Write a speech explaining to people in your village why it's a good idea to be friendly to the newcomers."

During an Anglo-Saxon feast, the king would sometimes give out gifts to men who were loyal to him. These gifts could include treasure that they had won after a successful battle.

Extension Idea

Pupils could discuss whether they would rather attend an Anglo-Saxon feast or a modern day party and why.

Daily Life for Anglo-Saxons

Anglo-Saxons: Activity Book p.18-19

Extension Idea

Pupils could split up into groups and create a short play to show what a day might have been like for an ordinary Anglo-Saxon.

Pupils could be reminded that water from rivers wasn't usually drunk directly in Anglo-Saxon times because it was often <u>dirty</u>.

Extension Idea

There are lots of recipes for pottage on the Internet. Pupils could have a go at making pottage themselves or sampling some that's been made for them.

Pupil Guidance:

"Remember, the Anglo-Saxons didn't have electricity or modern kitchen appliances."

18

Daily Life for Anglo-Saxons

Day-to-day life was tough for ordinary Anglo-Saxons. They didn't have many of the luxuries that we have today. Read page 18 of the Study Book to find out more.

How did Anglo-Saxons get their <u>water</u>? Write or draw your answer in the box.

If an Anglo-Saxon wanted water, they would have had to go and collect it from a nearby river, stream or well. (Pupils may have given their answer as a drawing.)

List <u>three</u> things that Anglo-Saxons used <u>rivers</u> for. Put a tick (✓) next to the things we still use rivers for in Britain today.

1) *water for washing / cooking* ☐
2) *travelling by boat* ☑
3) *powering water mills* ☑

Read page 19 of the Study Book. The Anglo-Saxons often ate <u>pottage</u>.

Imagine you are an Anglo-Saxon making some pottage for your dinner. Which <u>three</u> of the following tasks would <u>not</u> be part of the recipe? Circle the correct answers.

Dig up a turnip from the garden.

Wash a leek under the tap.

Grind up some beans.

Take some butter out of the fridge.

Chop an onion.

Heat some water on the electric stove.

Anglo-Saxons often ate bread with their pottage. How do you think they got their bread?

I think they baked it themselves.

Extension Idea

Pupils could keep a food diary. They could compare the food they eat with the sorts of foods that an Anglo-Saxon would have eaten. They could discuss how and why the foods they eat are different.

Pupils may also say that items were traded for bread.

Daily Life for Anglo-Saxons: National Curriculum Aims
- Know how people's lives have shaped Britain.
- Understand similarity and difference and use them to draw contrasts.

19

Most Anglo-Saxon houses didn't have chimneys. How could this have caused problems for the people living in the house?

It made the house smokey. / It meant that poisonous gases from the fire couldn't escape.

This picture shows some Anglo-Saxon household objects that have been found by archaeologists.

These objects are from the Ashmolean Museum in Oxford. You may find their website useful when doing research.

For each of the objects A, B and C, write down what you think the object is, and what the Anglo-Saxons might have used it for.

I think A is a *bucket*

I think it would have been used for *carrying water / beer*

I think B is a *bowl*

I think it would have been used for *eating from*

I think C is a *jar / cooking pot*

I think it would have been used for *storing food / cooking*

Pupil Guidance:

"You're not expected to know exactly what these objects were used for — just come up with sensible ideas. Do we use any similar looking objects today?"

Carrying water is a suitable answer here, but archaeologists think this bucket is actually too small to have been used in this way. Instead, they think it might have been used to carry beer or mead at feasts. Accept any sensible suggestions as answers for this question.

Would you rather live in modern-day times or in Anglo-Saxon times? Explain your answer.

I would rather live in

because

"I know what daily life was like for the Anglo-Saxons, including how they got water and what they ate."

Pupils can say that they would rather live in modern or Anglo-Saxon times, as long as they give a good reason.

Anglo-Saxon Religions

Anglo-Saxons: Activity Book p.20-21

20

Anglo-Saxon Religions

When the Angles and Saxons first invaded Britain, they worshipped Pagan gods. Pagan religions have different gods and goddesses for different things.

Tiw was a Pagan god of war.

Draw a picture of what you think Tiw might have looked like.

Suggested Scaffolding:

Tiw is often drawn as a strong man with a large sword and shield.

Extension Idea

Pupils could write a story involving Tiw or illustrate one in the style of a cartoon strip. The story could involve other gods or goddesses or mythical creatures such as elves and dragons.

The Anglo-Saxons did a lot of fighting.

Why do you think they had a god of war?

I think the Anglo-Saxons had a god of war because fighting and winning battles was very important to them. They thought their god of war would help them win battles.

Early Anglo-Saxons in Britain had Pagan gods and goddesses of things that were important to them.

Apart from war, write down two things you think the Anglo-Saxons might have had a god or goddess of.

1) *farming*
2) *wealth*

There is a wide range of possible answers to this question. Some Pagan Anglo-Saxon gods that we know about include the goddess of love, the god of thunder, the god of light and the goddess of springtime.

Anglo-Saxon Religions: National Curriculum Aims

- Understand the connections between religious and social history.
- Understand how Britain has been influenced by the wider world.
- Know the history of Britain as a chronological narrative.
- Create structured accounts.

21

Christianity survived in some parts of Britain,
even after the Angles and Saxons invaded.

Where in Britain did Christianity still survive? Why did it survive?
Use page 20 of the Study Book to help you.

Christianity still survived in *Wales*

because *the Saxons had not settled there.*

Augustine was a monk who was sent on a mission to Britain.
Read pages 20 and 21 of the Study Book to find out about this.

Now imagine that you're Augustine, and that you are planning
your mission to Britain. Write down what your mission is
and a step-by-step plan for how you're going to carry it out.

Try to include as much detail as possible in your plan.

My mission: *Convert the Anglo-Saxons to Christianity.*

My step-by-step plan:

1. Travel to Kent.

2. Visit King Aethelbert of Kent, who is Pagan.

3. Speak to the King's wife, Bertha, who is Christian.

4. Get Bertha's help to convert Aethelbert to Christianity.

"I understand how the Pagan Anglo-Saxons
were converted to Christianity."

Suggested Scaffolding:

Augustine's mission was to: 'Go to Britain and convert the Anglo-Saxons to Christianity'.

Pupil Guidance:

"Think about the people Augustine visited when he came to Britain. Who did he need help from to carry out his plan?"

These are the main points that pupils should have covered in their answers. Higher ability pupils may have included more imaginative details, for example: 'Buy Bertha a gift to help win her friendship' or 'Report back to Pope Gregory on my progress'. Pupils should make the separate steps in their plans clear.

Anglo-Saxon Law

Anglo-Saxons: Activity Book p.22-23

Pupil Guidance:

"As in Anglo-Saxon times, punishments today can include fines. Today, people can also be sent to prison or made to help out in society by doing activities such as picking up litter or cleaning public buildings."

The 50 shilling fine for killing a freeman was part of a system called 'weregild', or 'human-money'. There were different fines imposed for inflicting different injuries, right down to one shilling for a bruise.

Before the system of weregild, injuries often started 'blood feuds'. A person who was injured would take vengeance on his enemy. Since he often did more to the enemy than the enemy had done to him, this escalated the situation, and things got worse. Sometimes whole families were killed.

22

Anglo-Saxon Law

Anglo-Saxon law wasn't always written down. It used to be passed around by word of mouth. King Aethelbert published the first written law. Here are some of the first laws that he wrote down:

> If a man steals from the king, he must pay the king nine times what he stole.
> If anyone kills a freeman, they must pay a fine of 50 shillings to the king.
> If a man breaks into a house, he must pay 6 shillings to the owner of the house.

A shilling was just an amount of money.

Write down three of your own laws for modern-day Britain.
Include the punishment you think there should be for breaking each law.

1) *If you steal something from a shop, you should pay the shopkeeper twice what the object you stole was worth.*

2) *If you break something belonging to someone else, you must replace it and pay back half what it is worth.*

3) *If you drop litter in a public place, you must spend a day helping to clean and pick up litter in that place.*

Use page 22 of the Study Book to help you decide whether the statements below are true or false. Tick the correct box for each statement.

The witan was a group of important men, who were responsible for discussing crime. — True ✓ False ☐

An Anglo-Saxon criminal was called a gemot. — True ☐ False ✓

Oath-helpers would swear the suspect was innocent. — True ✓ False ☐

Criminals could be tried at a thousands court. — True ☐ False ✓

Extension Idea

Pupils could discuss whether the system of weregild was better than allowing blood feuds to develop.

Anglo-Saxon Law: National Curriculum Aims
- Create structured accounts.
- Understand the achievements and follies of mankind.
- Understand change.

Read pages 22 and 23 of the Study Book. Now imagine that you're an <u>official</u> at an Anglo-Saxon <u>court</u>. A man has been brought to the court and is suspected of having stolen some sheep from another man.

The suspect doesn't have an oath-breaker, so you need to decide what punishment will be suitable for him if he is found guilty.

Suggest a suitable <u>punishment</u> for the crime.

He should have to pay a fine. / He should have a (named) body part chopped off. / He should be drowned/beheaded.

Write down <u>why</u> you think that this is a suitable punishment for the crime.

....

....

The court needs to decide if the man is <u>guilty or not</u>.

Describe <u>two ordeals</u> that the court might use to decide if the man is guilty.

1) *The suspect has to pick up an object from the bottom of a cauldron of boiling water. If the blisters on his hands heal, he is innocent. If the blisters become infected, he is guilty.*

2) *The suspect is tied up and thrown into a river or a lake. If he is guilty, he will float on top of the water. If he is innocent, he will sink.*

....

"I know how criminals in Anglo-Saxon times were tried and punished."

There were no prisons in Anglo-Saxon times, so 'He should go to prison' is not a suitable answer here. Pupils may go into more detail, e.g. by suggesting the <u>amount</u> the criminal should be fined.

There is a wide range of possible answers here. Pupils may link the punishment they have chosen to how severe they think the crime is.

Extension Idea
Pupils could discuss <u>how</u> and <u>why</u> the punishments for crimes today are different to Anglo-Saxon punishments. They could also discuss why crimes need to be punished and whether they think Anglo-Saxon or modern punishments work better.

Suggested Scaffolding:
"For each ordeal, you should include:
- *what's supposed to happen if the suspect is innocent,*
- *what's supposed to happen if the suspect is guilty."*

Extension Idea
Pupils could invent a crime, such as the theft of an animal or some food, and re-enact an Anglo-Saxon court case to try the suspected thief. Pupils could take the roles of officals, the suspect, the victim and oath-helpers.

The Top of Society

Anglo-Saxons: Activity Book p.24-25

Pupil Guidance:

"Think about the sort of clothes a bretwalda might have worn and what sort of weapons he might have had. The picture on page 24 of the Study Book shows what some high-ranking Anglo-Saxons might have looked like."

Pupils may have different ideas about what a bretwalda would have looked like, but they should have recognised that bretwaldas were powerful and wealthy. They should have tried to show this in their picture and made it clear through their labelling.

At this time kings were often not the direct descendants of the previous king. Sometimes there were several rival claimants for the throne, and then there was often trouble, as everyone wanted the job!

24

The Top of Society

At any one time, there were multiple Anglo-Saxon kings, one for each kingdom.

Complete the sentences below using information from page 24 of the Study Book.

The word bretwalda means _Britain-ruler_

The bretwalda was the most powerful _king in Britain at_

any one time.

Draw a picture in the box of what you think a <u>bretwalda</u> might have looked like.

<u>Label</u> your picture to explain why you've drawn your bretwalda the way you have.

<u>Ealdormen</u>, <u>aethelings</u>, <u>kings</u> and <u>thegns</u> were all ranks at the top of Anglo-Saxon society. You can read all about them on pages 24 and 25 of the Study Book.

Write out these ranks in order from 1 to 4. <u>Number 1</u> should be the <u>highest rank</u>. <u>Number 4</u> should be the <u>lowest rank</u>. One has been done for you.

Ealdorman	Aetheling	King	Thegn

1) _King_

2) _Aetheling_

3) _Ealdorman_

4) _Thegn_

Extension Idea

Ask pupils to write a <u>job advert</u> for a king for the kingdom of Wessex. They should set out the requirements for the job to make sure they get the right person to apply... and it's probably best <u>not</u> to mention that the successful applicant stands a good chance of ending up dead!

The Top of Society: National Curriculum Aims

- Know how people's lives have shaped Britain.
- Understand the connections between social and political history.
- Create structured accounts.

25

A <u>fact file</u> is a <u>collection of facts</u> about a particular topic. Imagine you've been asked to write a fact file for a website on the Anglo-Saxons. Use page 25 of the Study Book to write a fact file about <u>ealdormen</u> OR a fact file about <u>thegns</u>.

E.g. Ealdormen looked after areas of land in a kingdom. They were chosen by the king. They could be aethelings. They were part of the witan.

Thegns were military men. They served the king or an ealdorman. They acted as soldiers or bodyguards. They were given their own land in payment.

> Pupils may have given additional facts. For example, thegns made sure roads and bridges were repaired and built military buildings in times of peace. The best fact files will include at least four facts on either ealdormen or thegns. Pupils may have chosen to present their facts in, e.g. a numbered list.

In Anglo-Saxon times, the <u>witan</u> chose a <u>new king</u> when the old one died.

Imagine you're part of the witan. The old king has died and you have to choose a new king. Who would you choose from the men below and why?

> **Pupil Guidance:**
> *"Remember, when a king died, the new king would have been picked from the king's relatives, known as the aethelings."*

Cenric — a thegn who has led many men into battle.

Godric — an old and wise bishop.

Dudda — the king's brother who is known to take bribes and steal.

Oswald — an ealdorman who is a strong warrior.

Eadgar — an aetheling who is intelligent but cowardly.

Wilfred — the king's cousin who is brave and a good leader.

I would choose Wilfred

because he is an aetheling, so he could become king. Also, someone who is brave and a good leader would make a good king.

> Any answer is acceptable here as long as pupils back it up with a good reason. If they haven't picked an aetheling, they should say why. If they have, they should try to say why they picked that aetheling in particular.

"I understand the different ranks of people at the top of Anglo-Saxon society."

> **Extension Idea**
> Pupils could be asked to design a campaign poster or write a speech to persuade the rest of the witan why the person they've chosen is the best for the job.

Extension Idea

Pupils could discuss how we decide on the leader of the country today. What is the difference between how the Queen was chosen and the Prime Minister?

Beowulf and Sutton Hoo

Anglo-Saxons: Activity Book p.26-27

Suggested Scaffolding:

Pupils could be shown a picture to base their poem on, for example the image of King Arthur on page 13 of the Study Book. Alternatively, they could choose an image themselves from a book they've read.

Anglo-Saxon poetry uses alliteration over a line with a break, e.g. 'The foul fiend trod / the tiled floor'. Higher ability pupils could try to make their poem alliterative.

26

Beowulf and Sutton Hoo

Beowulf is an Anglo-Saxon poem. It's about a brave hero and some scary monsters.

Write a short poem describing a king or queen, a hero, or a monster.

You can write your poem however you like — Beowulf doesn't rhyme, but that doesn't mean yours can't!

> A dragon lived inside a cave,
> He guarded lots of treasure.
> The shiny coins and jewels he owned,
> He counted at his leisure.
> His teeth were sharp, his claws were long,
> His scales were strong as steel.
> And no one would dare wake him up,
> Or they'd become his meal!

Some characters from Beowulf are written below. Sort them into the table to show whether you think they could appear in history or are just works of fantasy.

Works of fantasy are things that are made up.

A rich king   A giant monster   A heroic warrior   A dragon

An evil king who betrays his people   A beautiful and wise queen

History	Fantasy
a heroic warrior an evil king who betrays his people a beautiful and wise queen a rich king	a giant monster a dragon

Extension Idea

Pupils could try and think of some stories that are set in modern day Britain. These could be from books, films or TV programmes. For each story, they could think of aspects of the story that could be real, and aspects that could only be works of fantasy.

Beowulf and Sutton Hoo: National Curriculum Aims

- Create written narratives.
- Understand methods of historical enquiry.
- Understand how evidence is used to make historical claims.

27

Sutton Hoo is an Anglo-Saxon burial site. The person who was buried in the ship at Sutton Hoo was buried with all his precious treasures.

> Write down three objects that are precious to you.

Three objects that are precious to me are my bike / my games console / my teddy bear / my photographs / my computer.

One of the greatest finds at Sutton Hoo was a helmet, shown on page 27 of the Study Book. When it was new, it would have been covered with detailed patterns.

> Draw your own design for a helmet that might have been worn by an Anglo-Saxon king.

We can use the evidence from Sutton Hoo and the poem 'Beowulf' to find out what life might have been like for kings living during the Anglo-Saxon period.

> Read page 27 of the Study Book, then read the statements below. Tick the box that best describes what the evidence at Sutton Hoo shows about 'Beowulf'.

Sutton Hoo shows that everything in Beowulf happened. ☐

Sutton Hoo shows that nothing in Beowulf happened. ☐

Sutton Hoo shows that parts of Beowulf might be accurate. ☑

"I understand the links between Beowulf and Sutton Hoo, and what this teaches us about Anglo-Saxon life."

It is believed that the king who was buried at Sutton Hoo was Raedwald, king of East Anglia.

Pupil Guidance:

"It's thought that, when the Sutton Hoo helmet was new, it was covered with lots of detailed pictures and patterns. Some of the pictures showed Anglo-Saxon warriors in battle scenes."

Extension Idea

Pupils could research what other treasures were found at Sutton Hoo. They could choose a piece of treasure to make a model of, using papier mâché or card, paint and tin foil.

The Sutton Hoo treasures are now on display at the British Museum in London. You may find their website helpful when doing research.

Extension Idea

Ask pupils to write a newspaper report about the Sutton Hoo ship burial. They should think about what they might have been able to see at the burial, and comment on the grave goods.

The Bottom of Society

Anglo-Saxons: Activity Book p.28-29

Pupil Guidance:

"There are lots of tools an Anglo-Saxon farmer would have used at the top of page 28 of the Study Book."

The tools shown on page 28 of the Study Book are from the <u>Hurbuck hoard</u>. The hoard contained the blades from tools that would have been used to cut grain, as well as an axe head and a tool called an adze, used for woodwork.

Pupils may give different reasons for why the tool is important to them. They may say that it allows them to grow food for their family or to earn a living.

Anglo-Saxons who were starving could <u>choose</u> to sell themselves into slavery. Britons who were captured or Anglo-Saxon criminals had no choice about whether they would become slaves.

28

The Bottom of Society

<u>Ceorls</u> were near the bottom of Anglo-Saxon society. Most ceorls were <u>farmers</u>. Read page 28 of the Study Book.

Pretend you are an Anglo-Saxon ceorl. Draw a <u>tool</u> you use for farming. Write down why this tool is <u>important</u> to you.

This tool is important to me

because ....

....

....

There were different ranks of ceorl.

List <u>two</u> jobs that a high-ranking ceorl might have had to do.

1) *Carry messages*

2) *Deal with visitors to his master's house*

Read page 29 of the Study Book.

Each of the people below became a <u>slave</u>. Draw a line to match each person to the speech bubble that's most likely to describe how they became a slave.

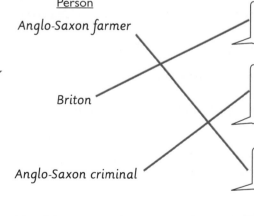

Person

Anglo-Saxon farmer

Briton

Anglo-Saxon criminal

I was captured by the Saxons during a battle.

I couldn't afford to pay the fine to the family of a man I killed.

I was starving and couldn't grow enough food.

The Bottom of Society: National Curriculum Aims

- Know how people's lives have shaped Britain.
- Understand similarity and difference.

29

Most Anglo-Saxon slaves spent their whole lives as slaves. Some were lucky enough to be <u>freed</u>.

Write down <u>two</u> ways in which a slave could be freed.

1) *They could buy their freedom.*

2) *They could be set free when their masters died.*

Read the following statements. Write each statement in the correct column in the table to show whether it describes <u>ceorls</u> or <u>slaves</u>. Use pages 28 and 29 of the Study Book to help you.

They were free.   *They could be sold.*

They weren't allowed to marry.   *They had personal rights.*

Ceorls	Slaves
They were free *They had personal rights*	*They weren't allowed to marry* *They could be sold*

Think about all the different ranks you've learnt about on pages 24 to 29 of the Study Book.

Which rank would you most like to be if you were an Anglo-Saxon? Why?

If I were an Anglo-Saxon, I would most like to be ....

because ....

....

....

"I understand the different ranks of people at the bottom of Anglo-Saxon society."

Pupils could also write that slaves were bought and freed by churchmen.

Extension Idea

Pupils could discuss whether they think slaves were as important a part of Anglo-Saxon society as higher ranks. They could discuss what Anglo-Saxon Britain might have been without a king, without thegns or without slaves.

Suggested Scaffolding:

"The ranks you can choose from are:
- *Bretwalda*
- *King*
- *Aetheling*
- *Ealdorman*
- *Thegn*
- *Ceorl*
- *Slave*"

Extension Idea

Pupils could imagine they were slaves whose master had died and set them free. Ask pupils in pairs to act out a conversation two slaves might have the night before they 'owned themselves' once more. They would certainly be excited, but would they also be worried about their future?

Anglo-Saxon Women

Anglo-Saxons: Activity Book p.30-31

30

Anglo-Saxon Women

Anglo-Saxon men and women tended to do different jobs. For example, the men would do most of the farming. Women would look after the children. Today, many men and women do the same jobs.

Write down some jobs that both men and women do today, both inside and outside of the home.

Some jobs that both men and women do today are cleaning / cooking / ironing / hoovering / doctors / shop keepers politicians / electricians / bus drivers

Anglo-Saxon women had to make all of their clothes themselves.

How is this different to how you get your clothes today?

Today I don't have to make my own clothes. I can go and buy them from a shop.

Read page 30 of the Study Book. Draw a piece of equipment that an Anglo-Saxon woman would have used to help her make clothes. Write down what the piece of equipment is called and what it was used for.

This piece of equipment is called a loom
It was used for weaving threads together to make cloth.

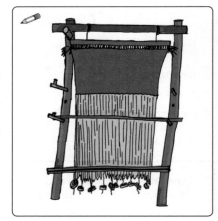

A wide range of answers is possible for this question.

Extension Idea

Pupils could use books or the Internet to research some clothes that an Anglo-Saxon woman might have made. They could then design an Anglo-Saxon-style outfit for themselves. Ordinary Anglo-Saxon women and girls would have worn long dresses. Men and boys would have worn a thick tunic over a pair of trousers. Richer men and women would have worn more decorative clothes. Pupils may need help finding suitable websites for their research.

Anglo-Saxon Women: National Curriculum Aims

- Understand how people's lives have shaped Britain.
- Understand similarity and difference and use them to draw contrasts.
- Understand change.
- Create written narratives.

31

Anglo-Saxon women had different ranks in society.

Read page 31 of the Study Book, then decide whether the statements below are true or false. Tick the correct box for each statement.

Both poor and rich women were responsible for housekeeping. True ✓ False ☐

Rich women sometimes had to organise large social events. True ✓ False ☐

Women weren't allowed to rule kingdoms. True ☐ False ✓

Aethelfleda was a poor farmer. True ☐ False ✓

Most Anglo-Saxon women were married. A peace-weaver had an arranged marriage. You can find out more about peace-weavers on page 31 of the Study Book.

Acha is 12 and she is a peace-weaver. She is marrying Osfrid, a young man from a rival tribe. Pretend you are Acha. Write down how you feel about the marriage.

✎ I'm worried about marrying Osfrid. I don't think he'll like me because I'm from a rival tribe.
I think marriage will be boring too!
I'd much rather play games with my sister.

Now pretend you're Acha's father. How do you feel about Acha's marriage?

✎ I'm pleased Acha is marrying Osfrid and I'm confident it will keep the peace between our two tribes. I hope Osfrid and his family look after her though.

"I understand what Anglo-Saxon women's lives were like." 👍✓ 🤚✓ 👎✓

Extension Idea

Pupils could write a diary entry about a day in the life of an Anglo-Saxon woman. They could choose to write from the perspective of an ordinary farmer's wife or a wealthy noblewoman.

Pupil Guidance:

"How would you feel if you had to get married at 12? How do you think Acha might feel at marrying someone her family has argued with in the past?"

Pupils may write a variety of answers for these two questions. They may recognise that Acha and her father might have different views on the marriage.

Pupil Guidance:

"Think about why Acha's father has arranged this marriage for her."

Anglo-Saxon Children

Anglo-Saxons: Activity Book p.32-33

32

Anglo-Saxon Children

Anglo-Saxon children were expected to work and help their parents run the home and farm from a very young age.

This is what a typical day for an Anglo-Saxon boy might have been like:

5:00 am:	Get up. Fetch and chop wood for the fire in the house.
5:30 am:	Have breakfast of bread and weak ale.
6:00 am:	Feed the animals and fetch water for them from the stream.
10:00 am:	Return home for a mid-morning meal of bread and pottage.
11:00 am:	Work on the farm, weeding and ploughing the fields.
6:00 pm:	Return home for an evening meal. Listen to stories and play games before going to bed.

Write down what a typical day for <u>you</u> is like.

7:30 am: Wake up. Have breakfast of cereal and toast.

9:00 am: Start school. Learn history, maths and English.

12:00 pm: Fish and chips for lunch. Play football in the playground during lunch break.

1:00 pm : More lessons at school, followed by P.E.

3:00 pm: Go home and do homework.

5:00 pm: Attend a music lesson.

6:00 pm: Have an evening meal and watch TV before bed.

Write <u>two</u> ways in which your day is <u>different</u> from an Anglo-Saxon child's day.

1) I wake up later than Anglo-Saxon children.

2) I go to school instead of working on a farm.

Suggested Scaffolding:

Pupils could choose to write about:

- a school day
- a weekend
- a day during the school holidays.

There is a variety of possible answers to this question. Pupils should write about a full day from their lives, including the times at which they do different activities.

There are other possible answers to this question. For example, children may say that they watch TV, which Anglo-Saxon children didn't do.

Extension Idea

Pupils could write a story about an Anglo-Saxon child. They could set their story in Anglo-Saxon times or they could write about what might happen if an Anglo-Saxon child were to time travel to the present day!

Anglo-Saxon Children: National Curriculum Aims

- Create structured accounts.
- Understand how people's lives have shaped Britain.
- Understand similarity and difference and use them to draw contrasts.
- Understand change.

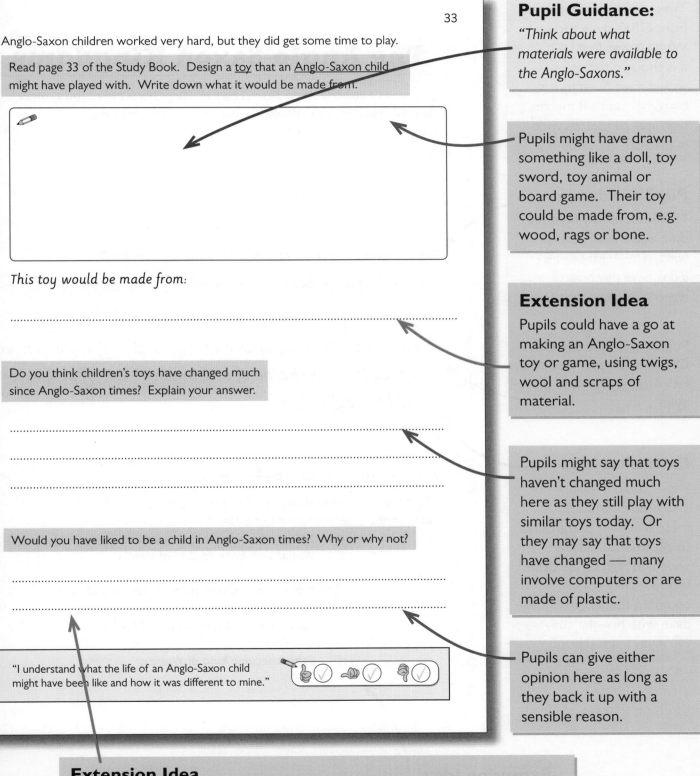

Anglo-Saxon children worked very hard, but they did get some time to play.

Read page 33 of the Study Book. Design a toy that an Anglo-Saxon child might have played with. Write down what it would be made from.

This toy would be made from:

....

Do you think children's toys have changed much since Anglo-Saxon times? Explain your answer.

....

....

....

Would you have liked to be a child in Anglo-Saxon times? Why or why not?

....

....

"I understand what the life of an Anglo-Saxon child might have been like and how it was different to mine."

Pupil Guidance:

"Think about what materials were available to the Anglo-Saxons."

Pupils might have drawn something like a doll, toy sword, toy animal or board game. Their toy could be made from, e.g. wood, rags or bone.

Extension Idea

Pupils could have a go at making an Anglo-Saxon toy or game, using twigs, wool and scraps of material.

Pupils might say that toys haven't changed much here as they still play with similar toys today. Or they may say that toys have changed — many involve computers or are made of plastic.

Pupils can give either opinion here as long as they back it up with a sensible reason.

Extension Idea

Discuss with pupils whether they think Anglo-Saxon children stayed 'children' for as long as children do today. Think about how long they studied for, and the age at which they were expected to do 'grown-up' things.

The Anglo-Saxon Kingdoms

Anglo-Saxons: Activity Book p.34-35

These are measurements from Offa's dyke today. When it was first built, it is thought that it would have been much bigger — up to 8 metres high and 20 metres wide in places.

Pupil Guidance:

"Think about how hard the dyke would have been to build. The Anglo-Saxons didn't have mechanical diggers or power tools."

Pupils might also say that Offa would have needed a lot of <u>money</u> to build the dyke.

Extension Idea

Pupils could measure out 19.5 metres and 2.5 metres in their playground to get a sense of how wide and high Offa's dyke is now. They could compare the length of the dyke with how far they live away from school.

34

The Anglo-Saxon Kingdoms

<u>Mercia</u> was a powerful Anglo-Saxon kingdom. King Offa of Mercia had a barrier built between Mercia and Wales. The barrier is called <u>Offa's dyke</u>.

Here are some facts about Offa's dyke today:

> Widest point of the dyke = 19.5 metres
> Highest point of the dyke = 2.5 metres
> Length of the dyke = 150 miles

Page 34 of the Study Book has a picture of Offa's dyke being built.

How do you think building the dyke showed that Offa was a powerful king?

Building the dyke showed Offa was powerful because the dyke would have to have been built by hand. Offa would have needed to be in charge of and organise lots of people to build the dyke.

Page 35 of the Study Book describes how the kingdom of <u>Wessex</u> became very powerful during the 9th century.

Read the statements below and number them <u>1 to 4</u> to show the <u>order</u> in which they happened.

4	*Wiglaf won back control of Mercia.*
2	*Egbert won control of Essex, Sussex and Kent.*
3	*Egbert defeated King Wiglaf of Mercia.*
1	*Egbert became king of Wessex.*

Extension Idea

Pupils could draw out these events on a timeline to show when they happened. Their timelines should start at AD 800.

The Anglo-Saxon Kingdoms: National Curriculum Aims

- Understand the history of Britain as a chronological narrative.
- Understand the achievements of mankind.
- Understand change.

35

When King Egbert was very powerful, he started to make his own <u>coins</u>.

Look at the coin shown on page 35 of the Study Book.
How is the design similar to that of the coins we use today?

King Egbert's coin is similar to coins we use today because
it has the picture and name of the ruler on one side of it.

Pupils might pick up on other similarities such as the <u>shape</u>.

Imagine you're the ruler of an Anglo-Saxon kingdom. Design your <u>own coin</u>. Draw each side of your coin in the circles below.

Anglo-Saxon coins usually had the face and name of the ruler on one side. On the other side, there could be a pattern, a religious symbol, or even an animal!

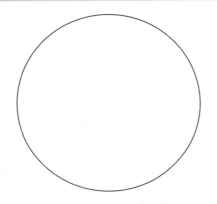
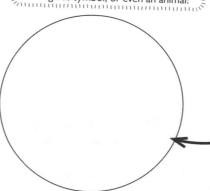

Suggested Scaffolding:

Give pupils some modern coins to look at for inspiration.

In your own words, write down <u>how</u> Egbert was able to start making his own coins. Use page 35 of the Study Book to help you.

Egbert won control of London and Canterbury. These
places had buildings where coins were made. Egbert was
able to make his own coins in these buildings.

Suggested Scaffolding:

'Egbert was able to start making coins when he took control of London and Canterbury.'

Higher ability pupils might add that Egbert had control of London and Canterbury by <u>AD 829</u>.

"I know that Anglo-Saxon Britain was split up into kingdoms and that the kingdoms fought for power."

The Golden Age

Anglo-Saxons: Activity Book p.36-37

Suggested Scaffolding:

"*Some items that were found in the Staffordshire hoard include:*

- *crosses*
- *helmets/shields*
- *sword hilts.*"

Pupils should label their object as being made of gold. They may also label precious stones on their object.

Some of the stones in the Staffordshire hoard are garnets. It's thought that they could have come from India or Sri Lanka.

Extension Idea

The Staffordshire Hoard tells us about the things rich people valued then. How are those different from the things that people spend a lot of money on nowadays? Why might this be?

36

The Golden Age

Read the information about the Staffordshire hoard on page 36 of the Study Book. The Staffordshire hoard contains items made of precious materials.

Design an object that might have been found in the Staffordshire hoard. Label your object to show what it's made from.

The Staffordshire hoard contains precious stones that are thought to come from abroad. What might this provide evidence of?

It provides evidence that the Anglo-Saxons in Britain were wealthy and might have traded with foreign countries.

The Lindisfarne Gospels are an example of an Anglo-Saxon illuminated text.

Read page 37 of the Study book and decide whether the statements below are true or false. Tick the correct box for each statement.

Lindisfarne priory was built on Holy Island. — True ☑ False ☐

The Lindisfarne Gospels were written by nuns. — True ☐ False ☑

The Lindisfarne Gospels are illustrated with patterns and pictures. — True ☑ False ☐

The Lindisfarne Gospels would have been cheap to make. — True ☐ False ☑

Extension Idea

Pupils could create their own illustrated texts. They could start by writing out a line from one of their favourite books, and then illustrating it with decorative borders and colourful pictures.

The Golden Age: National Curriculum Aims
- Understand the history of Britain as a chronological narrative.
- Understand the achievements of mankind.
- Understand how evidence is used to make historical claims.
- Understand change.

The Lindisfarne Gospels are in Latin, but the Anglo-Saxons also wrote in Old English. Some of the words we use today come from Old English.

Below are some modern <u>English</u> words and some <u>Old English</u> words. Draw lines to match each English word to the Old English word you think it came from.

<u>English words:</u>   <u>Old English words:</u>

cheese   dohtor   cu

daughter   cow   bridd

bird   cese

This photograph shows an Anglo-Saxon building.

What do you think this building is?

A church...

What is this building made from? Where do you think the Anglo-Saxons got this building material from? Use page 37 of the Study Book to help you.

This building is made from stone...

I think the Anglo-Saxons might have got this material from ...taking.......
apart old Roman buildings and settlements.

Write down <u>one</u> reason why the Anglo-Saxons <u>wouldn't</u> have built this building when they first settled in Britain.

When the Anglo-Saxons first arrived in Britain they built
with wood not stone.

"I understand the ways in which Anglo-Saxon society became more advanced."

Extension Idea
Pupils could try to find out what other modern English words come from Old English. They could also try to find out what modern words come from Latin. For example
- 'armour' comes from the Latin 'arma'
- 'school' comes from the Latin 'schola'.

This is Escomb church in County Durham. It is thought to have been built at some point in the 7th century.

Pupil Guidance:
"Think about what the building is made from."

Pupils may also write that Anglo-Saxons wouldn't have built churches when they first moved to Britain as they were <u>Pagan</u>.

Defending Against Invaders

Anglo-Saxons: Activity Book p.38-39

Alfred the Great is the only king to have had 'the Great' attached to his name. Despite almost being pushed out of his kingdom of Wessex, he was rare in managing to mount a successful defence against the Vikings. Alfred also loved learning — something many Anglo-Saxons did not value!

Suggested Scaffolding:

"In your article, you should write about:

• the raiders from Scandinavia / Vikings

• the burhs' defensive walls and ditches

• how the burhs can help protect important buildings."

Pupil Guidance:

"Think about what the burhs were for and where the raiders were attacking."

Locations near ports, roads or rivers would also be sensible suggestions.

38

Defending Against Invaders

In the 9th century, King Alfred the Great ordered the first burhs to be built.

Read pages 38 and 39 of the Study Book. Imagine you are writing for an Anglo-Saxon newspaper. Write a short article about the burhs, including what they are, and why King Alfred has ordered them to be built.

The raiders from Scandinavia are now starting to cause serious trouble for Britain. They're stealing our treasure and they want to settle on our land.
But never fear, our courageous king has a plan!
King Alfred has ordered the first 'burhs' to be built.
Burhs are forts or towns surrounded by defensive walls and ditches. Our most important buildings can be built inside these burhs, making them easier to defend against attack.

The Burghal Hidage is a document that contains a list of some burhs in Britain.

Imagine you are building your own burh in Anglo-Saxon times. Complete the following sentences to describe where and how you would build it.

Use pages 38 and 39 of the Study Book to help you.

The place I would build my burh is on the coast near Hastings, in the south-east of England.

Extension Idea

Pupils could research Anglo-Saxon burhs using books or the Internet. Some are shown on the map on page 39 of the Study Book. Though most of the original Anglo-Saxon structures have now gone, in places such as Wallingford and Crickledale, parts of the defensive ditch has survived.

Defending Against Invaders: National Curriculum Aims

- Understand how Britain has been influenced by the wider world.
- Understand cause and consequence.
- Understand the achievements of mankind.

The materials I would use to build my burh are *stone and wood*

The buildings I would put in my burh are *mints and armouries*

I would call my burh *Fortisburh*

This is a picture of what my burh would look like.

> There's a picture of a burh on page 38 of the Study Book if you need some inspiration.

A wide variety of answers is possible here. In addition to those buildings described in the Study Book, higher ability pupils may identify other buildings that they think would be important or useful, for example churches.

Pupil Guidance:
"Think about the features your burh will need to defend it."

Extension Idea
Pupils could discuss why the features they've drawn would be useful in a burh.

Extension Idea
Pupils could make an information leaflet about their burh, persuading the Anglo-Saxons to live there.

"I know what Anglo-Saxon burhs were and why they were built."

Picture acknowledgements

Thumb illustration used throughout this book © iStockphoto.com.

p2 Geography photos / UIG via Getty Images.

p9 © iStockphoto.com / Khrizmo.

p16 Spectrum Colour Library / Heritage-Images.

p19 Ashmolean Museum, University of Oxford, UK / Bridgeman Images.

p37 © John Morrison / Alamy.